TEEN MENTAL HEALTH™

school violence and conflict resolution

Marilyn E. Smith,
Matthew Monteverde, and
Henrietta M. Lily

ROSEN
PUBLISHING®

New York

Published in 2013 by The Rosen Publishing Group, Inc.
29 East 21st Street, New York, NY 10010

Library of Congress Cataloging-in-Publication Data

Smith, Marilyn E.
School violence and conflict resolution/Marilyn E. Smith, Matthew Monteverde, Henrietta M. Lily.—1st ed.
    p. cm.—(Teen mental health)
Includes bibliographical references and index.
ISBN 978-1-4488-6891-9 (library binding)
1. School violence—United States—Prevention. 2. Conflict management—United States. I. Monteverde, Matthew. II. Lily, Henrietta M. III. Title.
LB3013.32.S63 2013
371.7'82—dc23

                                               2012003027

Manufactured in the United States of America

CPSIA Compliance Information: Batch #S12YA: For further information, contact Rosen Publishing, New York, New York, at 1-800-237-9932.

contents

School Violence and Conflict Resolution

chapter one

Violence: A Serious Problem in Schools

Federal statistics about the number of acts of school violence show that violence has been decreasing in U.S. schools. According to *Indicators of School Crime and Safety*, a 2010 joint report issued by the U.S. Department of Education and U.S. Department of Justice, the percentage of students who were victims of crime at school declined from 10 percent to almost 4 percent.

The peak of reported violence in schools occurred in the early 1990s, and, between 1992 and 1999,

A police helicopter leaves an Amish school after a crazed gunman attacked students in the Pennsylvania schoolhouse in 2006. Despite what the public might believe, statistics show that school violence has decreased since the late 1990s.

killings averaged a little more than 31 per year. This was perhaps best highlighted in April 1999 by the tragic shootings at Columbine High School in Littleton, Colorado, in which two troubled students opened fire on their classmates and the faculty. Twelve students and one teacher were killed before the gunmen committed suicide. The percentage of killings at schools from 2000 to 2009 averaged a little more than 19 per year.

Since the incident at Columbine, there have been other horrific shootings at U.S. schools. From 1999 to 2009, there were school shootings in at least thirty-two states and the District of Columbia. Canada has also had tragic school shootings in that time period, including in Alberta and Quebec.

Even colleges are not immune to school violence. On Monday, April 16, 2007, more than thirty people lost their lives in the deadliest school shooting in U.S. history. Cho Seung-Hui, a senior at Virginia Tech University, was identified as the gunman who killed thirty-two people at his school. At least ten other states have had incidents of school violence on their college campuses over the past decade.

Violence is defined as the use of force to cause damage or injury. School violence includes acts such as bullying, destroying expensive school equipment, and making threats against students and teachers. The most serious school violence of all occurs when actual physical harm is inflicted on students and teachers.

An Ongoing Challenge

What is happening to teens to make them so angry that they feel the need to hurt or kill? There are many possible reasons, such as bad grades, peer pressure, and problems at home, that may explain why teens turn to violence as a way of venting their frustrations.

Despite public support for gun control, access to guns is relatively easy. An increasing number of students carry guns and other types of weapons, such as box cutters, to school. Many teachers and students now believe that their schools are unsafe.

According to *Indicators of School Crime and Safety, 2010*, in school year 2008–2009, students ages twelve to

A school safety officer gathers information from a student who had his wallet stolen at school. U.S. schools reported that there were 619,000 thefts on school property involving students between the ages of twelve and eighteen in 2008–2009.

eighteen were victims of about one million nonfatal crimes away from school, including thefts (purse snatching, pick pocketing, and burglaries) and violent crimes (physical attacks and fights, without a weapon). Students in this same age range were victims of about 1.2 million nonfatal crimes at school (in the school building, on school property, or on the way to or from school)—619,000 thefts and 629,800 violent crimes.

The report also notes that in 2008 students, ages twelve to eighteen, were victims of four serious violent crimes (rape, sexual assault, robbery, and aggravated assault) per one thousand students at school and eight serious violent crimes per one thousand students away from school. There were twenty-two violent deaths of school-age youths (ages five to eighteen) between July 1, 2008 and June 30, 2009—fifteen were murders and seven were suicides. All the crime rates noted in the 2010 *Indicators* report are lower for that period than they were in the 2007–2008 school year.

The Centers for Disease Control and Prevention (CDC) released "Facts at a Glance" on youth violence in 2010. In the fact sheet, the CDC disclosed that in a national survey that was taken in 2009, 11.1 percent of the students said that they were in a physical fight at school in the twelve months before the survey. For the same time period, 7.7 percent said that they were threatened or injured with a weapon (gun, knife, or club) at school at least one time. Five percent of students also reported that they did not go to school one or more days in the thirty days before the survey because they did not feel safe at school. In addition, 5.6 percent of the youths reported that they carried a weapon on one or more days thirty days preceding the survey.

These statistics demonstrate how ordinary school violence has become. Students and teachers are all too commonly hit, stabbed, kicked, or shot. Sometimes a single student is the attacker, while at other times groups of students gang up on a teacher or another student. Although most of the aggressors are male, female students also carry weapons and act out physically.

Are Schools Safe Havens for Students?

According to the U.S. Department of Education and National Center for Education Statistics' report *Crime, Violence, Discipline, and Safety in U.S. Public Schools* (May 2011), during the 2009–2010 school year, per one thousand students, there were forty violent incidents in middle schools, twenty-one in primary schools, and twenty-one in high schools. The report also indicated there was a higher percentage (39 percent) of middle schools that said student bullying happened daily or at least once every week, compared to high schools or primary schools (at 20 percent each).

Many people used to think that school violence was a problem only in city schools. Violent crime also occurs in suburbs and rural towns. The criminals are troubled children, teens, and adults. The victims are usually students and teachers caught in the crossfire.

School Violence at Present

Since the late 1970s until around the mid to late 1990s, there had been a steady rise in school violence. The end of the first decade of the twenty-first century has seen a decline in many school violence statistics, including the number of students who said they carried a weapon on school property at least one day per month. One promising statistic is the one reported in *Indicators of School Crime and Safety, 2010* that between the 1999–2000 and 2007–2008 school years, there was a rise in the percentage of public schools that said they used safety and security measures to control access to school property during school hours. Such measures included requiring students and faculty to wear picture IDs or badges, using security cameras to monitor buildings, providing telephones in all classrooms, and requiring students to wear uniforms.

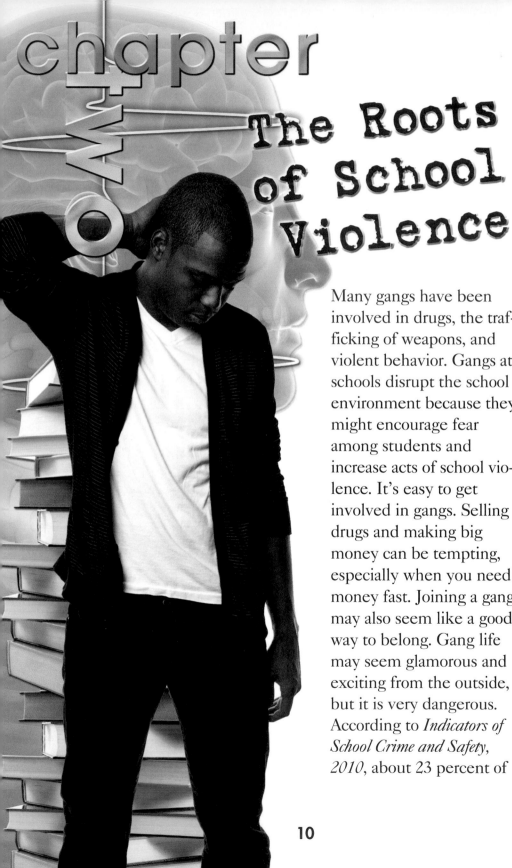

chapter TWO

The Roots of School Violence

Many gangs have been involved in drugs, the trafficking of weapons, and violent behavior. Gangs at schools disrupt the school environment because they might encourage fear among students and increase acts of school violence. It's easy to get involved in gangs. Selling drugs and making big money can be tempting, especially when you need money fast. Joining a gang may also seem like a good way to belong. Gang life may seem glamorous and exciting from the outside, but it is very dangerous. According to *Indicators of School Crime and Safety, 2010*, about 23 percent of

A dog that is trained to find guns, drugs, and alcohol sniffs student lockers at a middle school in Texas. The National Center for Education Statistics surveyed 3,476 U.S. schools in 2010 and found that 25 percent reported at least one incident of distribution, possession, or use of illegal drugs.

students surveyed in the 2007–2008 school year said that there were gangs in the school. The statistics show that there was an increase in 2005 from 2004 (24 from 21 percent), but there really hasn't been a change in recent years. Almost all gang members have either been the victims of violence or know someone who has. Many innocent bystanders have been victims as well.

Drug use by teens can also result in more violence at school. Someone who is high on drugs is more likely to behave impulsively, take risks, be angry, or hurt someone.

A drug addict may also steal from other students or teachers to pay for his or her habit.

Domestic Abuse

Many young people learn early in life that violence is acceptable. Children who grow up in homes where there is domestic abuse think violence is a normal part of life. Many violent people were abused when they were young. Young people who are abused or who see other family members abused often lash out themselves. They become violent because they are angry. Sometimes they use their fists because they don't know any other way to solve their problems.

The American Family

Some people believe that the rise in the number of single-parent families (according to the U.S. Bureau of Labor Statistics, there were 10,536,000 single-parent households in the United States in 2008) has led to an increase in school violence. They think that parents either don't have the energy or the desire to teach values to their kids.

Other people think that the breakdown of the family has led to violence by creating greater stress on parents and children. Many parents work long hours and have little time to spend with their families. Some teens become the caretakers of their younger siblings. The extra responsibility can be overwhelming, leading teens to feel frustrated and angry. Others feel unloved or unsupported because their parents don't pay attention to them. Some of them join gangs for friendship and excitement. Others become angry loners and may use violence against the people around them.

Getting a Gun

In 2009, the Youth Risk Behavior Surveillance System found that 5.9 percent of high school students carry a gun at least once a day. Furthermore, they estimate that 7.7 percent of high school students nationwide are injured or threatened with a weapon on school property one or more times at least once every year.

According to a 2005 report in the journal *Pediatrics*, 1.7 million American children live in a home that has

In a high school in Chicago, Illinois, all students use clear backpacks for safety and to speed up the searching process as they enter their school. Many schools are using a number of methods to reduce the chances of students bringing weapons to school.

unlocked and loaded firearms. Your parent or guardian may feel safer by having a gun at home. He or she needs to be smart about how that gun is stored and used in the home. To be safe at home, make sure that your gun-owning family member is a responsible person. If it is a brother or sister, let your parents or guardians know about the gun. If your sibling does not follow the rules, he or she should not have a gun. Check that he or she has unloaded the gun and locked it away. Bullets need to be stored separately from the gun and locked away. Ask an adult to help you make sure that your gun-owning relative follows these basic rules.

Although it may not be your gun, it may affect your life negatively in some way in the future. According to the Common Sense About Kids and Guns organization, about 75 percent of all gun-related accidents and suicides involving youths are committed with a gun found at home or at a relative's or friend's home. Ask yourself, "Does that gun add value to my life in any way?" Does it need to be a part of your life when it could potentially bring harm to it?

You may feel like the answer is yes, especially when you don't feel safe. Considering the Virginia Tech and Columbine massacres, you may think that school isn't a safe place at all. You may believe that if you had your own gun, you could live through a school shooting. Maybe you have even thought about taking a gun to school to feel safe. This is definitely not the answer.

Choose a better solution than taking a gun to school. Because of the Gun-Free School Zones Act, any student who is caught carrying a gun on school property is suspended for at least one year. The quick decision of taking a gun to school can set you back years, even if you had no intention of doing anything with it. If you feel like your school is unsafe, don't pick up a gun—pick up your pen. Start an antigun campaign. If you pick up a gun, it's twice as likely that you'll become a gun violence victim.

Watching for Warning Signs

There are signs that a fellow student—or yourself—may be headed for violence. According to the U.S. Department of Education, there are some early warning signs that indicate a teen is contemplating a dangerous activity. Some of these include when the student does the following:

- Socially withdraws
- Feels isolated
- Feels picked on
- Feels rejected
- Is already a victim of violence who is not coping with it
- Loses interest in performing well at school
- Expresses violence in writing or drawings
- Has uncontrollable anger
- Hits or bullies others
- Shows no tolerance to other ethnic or gender groups
- Is a practicing gang member
- Has made comments about being violent at school

It's important not to assume that if someone you know has some of these warning signs, he or she is going to carry out violence. A person may be displaying these

These students are physically bullying a rival on school property. One of the warning signs of students who might be headed toward violence is when they bully others.

signs because of a family tragedy or personal struggles that have nothing to do with the intention to do harm at school.

If you know someone who is showing these signs, don't approach him or her about it. Go to a trusted teacher or counselor and state that you want to talk about another student, but anonymously. Explain what you've observed and that you would like someone to talk to this peer before it's too late. By taking an active part on this student's behalf, you're making your school a safer place.

Don't Hesitate to Talk to Someone

There are immediate indicators that the chance of trouble is greatly increased or about to happen. Don't delay—talk to your counselor or teacher immediately if you observe the following indicators in someone's behavior:

- Physical fighting with peers
- Destruction of property
- Rage over the slightest things
- Threats—in great detail—about violence
- Consuming fascination with and possession of guns or other weapons
- Threats of suicide

Above all, if this person is planning to harm or kill others and is carrying a weapon, discreetly stop what you're doing and go to a guardian or adult. At this stage, law officers may come to make sure that this angered teen is not going to do anything with his or her gun.

You may feel scared about blowing the whistle, but be brave. This peer deserves help. He or she deserves to be stopped and given a healthy solution to coping with his or her problems. If at any point you find an actual gun somewhere, do not pick it up. Immediately call out for help from an adult or ask others to get an adult while you stand guard over it.

Media Violence and Entertainment

The entertainment industry has been widely criticized for sending the message to kids that violence is glamorous or exciting. But the media is not solely responsible for all of the violence in society. Society and the media feed off each another. If people didn't like to see violence, less of it would be shown.

In April 2008, the videotaped beating of a sixteen-year-old Florida girl by other teens who planned to post

Posting videos or photos of physical fights online is a growing problem with teens. Experts say this is one way that young and impressionable teens get attention for themselves. Experts believe that such actions can also lead to cyberbullying.

the video on YouTube and MySpace sparked national outrage and focused new attention on school violence and teen bullying. Eight teens faced charges of felony battery and false imprisonment for an "animalistic" attack on a fellow teen. Experts claim that, for teens, videotaping fights or using a cell phone's camera is a way of glorifying and flaunting conflicts, and many believe that teen violence and bullying are only going to worsen as it becomes easier for bullies to "perform on a worldwide stage."

MYTHS AND FACTS

Myth: Acts of school violence just keep increasing year after year.

Fact: According to figures reported in 2010 by the Departments of Education and Justice, the instances of school violence have continued to decline since their peak in the early 1990s. The percentage of students who reported being victims of school crime dropped from 10 percent to nearly 4 percent between the years 1995 and 2007. What has increased markedly is the number of reported cases of bullying.

Myth: Very few physical fights happen on school property involving female students.

Fact: The CDC reported in a 2009 national study representing young people in grades nine to twelve that 15.1 percent of male students and 6.7 percent of female students said they had been in a physical fight on school grounds in the twelve months prior to the survey.

Myth: No matter where the school is, violence in the classroom is a part of everyday life in America today and cannot be helped.

Fact: Although it's true that most schools have to deal with conflicts and violence, having a peer mediation or conflict resolution program in the school has proven to be extremely helpful in teaching kids how to communicate more effectively, practice active listening skills, and come up with more practical methods to solve conflicts and other disagreements.

19

chapter three

Cracking Down on School Violence

Students now encounter metal detectors on a regular basis—in their schools. More schools are installing metal detectors and hiring security guards. If a metal detector reveals that a student is carrying a weapon, serious action is taken. The weapon is confiscated and the authorities are contacted. Strict punishments have been imposed on students caught with weapons. Because of gun violence in the nation, the U.S. government and some states have passed strict weapons laws making the punishment for illegally carrying a gun much stiffer. In most U.S. states, it is illegal for anyone to sell a gun to a person under eighteen. In 1994, President Bill Clinton signed the Gun-Free School Zones Act. Under this law, a student caught possessing a weapon in school is expelled for one calendar year. Most schools today have zero-tolerance policies, which are regulations that punish students severely no matter how minor the offenses are. Zero-tolerance policies are aimed at students who cause school disruptions. These policies not only apply to weapons but also to fighting, gang activity, and drugs. In 2011, Representative Ron Paul of Texas introduced H.R. 2613 (Citizen's Protection Act of 2011) to repeal the Gun-Free School Zones Act and all its amendments. Paul and other gun advocates believe that the gun-free zone law is unconstitutional. The Citizen's Protection bill is currently in the House Committee on the Judiciary.

The Rights of Students and Get-Tough Measures

Some schools are trying to reduce gang-related violence by prohibiting students from wearing clothes that are often associated with gangs—for instance, certain types of hats, pants, sneakers, sweatshirts, and bandannas—to school.

Others believe a dress policy does not go to the heart of the problem, since gang-related violence makes up only a small part of the crime in most schools. They also think such rules unfairly restrict students' freedom of expression.

Police in Los Angeles, California, have a countersurveillance team and gang unit that work to fight gang violence in schools and communities.

Teachers want parents to become more involved in the schools. In some districts, parents have joined the "get-tough" movement; they patrol school hallways looking for weapons and violent behavior.

Some educators believe that parents need to take a more active role at home, too. They want parents to teach self-discipline to their children and support the school's disciplinary procedures.

Many people think the get-tough attitude helps. They believe students use violence simply because they think they can get away with it.

The Cell Phone, Smartphone, and Tablet Dispute

Educators, parents, and students are all trying to find ways to ensure that schools are safe. Many times these groups agree, but not always. One source of debate has been over the use of cell phones and other electronic devices at school. Some schools ban cell phones outright, saying that they disrupt classes and distract students. These schools

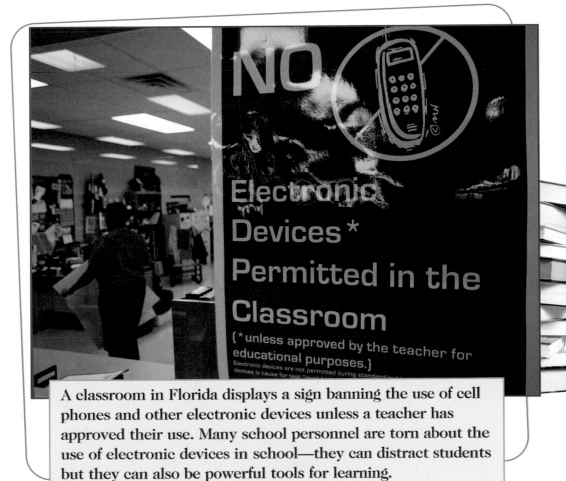

NO 🚫 Electronic Devices * Permitted in the Classroom

(*unless approved by the teacher for educational purposes.)

Electronic devices are not permitted during standard... devices is cause for test...

A classroom in Florida displays a sign banning the use of cell phones and other electronic devices unless a teacher has approved their use. Many school personnel are torn about the use of electronic devices in school—they can distract students but they can also be powerful tools for learning.

often also claim that smartphones can contribute to cheating if students use phones' text messaging or Web capabilities to help with assignments and exams.

Other schools allow students to carry cell phones and smartphones as long as the phones remain turned off on school property. Still other schools allow students to use cell phones more freely, provided they do so discreetly and according to school rules.

Some parents and students claim that schools must allow students to keep cell phones or smartphones in their possession for their own safety. More than just a convenience, they say that phones help teens and parents keep in contact in an emergency. Parents and students sometimes point to recent episodes of school violence as examples of how crucial cell phone communication could be in an emergency. However, make sure that both you and your parents know your school's cell phone policy.

10 Great Questions to Ask a Guidance Counselor

1. What should I do if someone threatens me at school?

2. Does school violence happen only in my state, or is it a national issue?

3. Is school violence an increasing problem since the horrible school shootings in the late 1990s?

4. Will bringing a weapon to school solve my problems if I feel unsafe?

5. What should I do if someone says they will hurt me after school?

6. How can I get my classmate to let me sit where I want in the lunchroom without fighting with her?

7. What should I do if someone I know brings a weapon on school property?

8. What are schools doing to prevent violence-related behavior at school?

9. How can I be open-minded enough to listen to another person's point of view when I have a conflict with that person?

10. Do you have any suggestions on how I could come up with a compromise to solve my conflict with my classmate?

Looking at Conflict Resolution

Conflict resolution is a way of handling conflicts by talking problems out—not fighting them out. The goal is not just to end a conflict, but also to solve the problem in a way that satisfies both sides. That's what "resolution" means: to deal with something successfully, to clear it up and find an answer.

In conflict resolution, both sides talk and listen to each other. Both get a chance to explain how they see the situation. This method allows each person involved to understand the other person's point of view. Then both can negotiate and discuss the problem to determine all possible solutions. They keep on talking until they come up with a solution that everyone can support.

Where and Why Do Conflicts Arise?

The list below explains the different kinds of conflict that you might come across in your lifetime:

- Intrapersonal: An internal conflict whose resolution will primarily affect your own life. For example,

A conflict between you and a friend about personal differences is a type of interpersonal conflict. Try to work toward understanding each other's point of view.

will you do drugs, or will you choose to be drug-free?

- Interpersonal: A conflict between two people. For example, you get in an argument with a classmate over where you will sit during lunch.
- Intergroup: A conflict between two groups. For example, an opponent might trip a player on your soccer team, and both teams argue over whether a foul was committed.
- Societal: A conflict in society. For example, conflicts due to skin color (racism) or gender (sexism).
- International: A conflict between two or more nations, such as a war.

Before you can solve a conflict, you have to understand what caused it. Conflicts usually concern these three basic issues:

Different Values—These conflicts have to do with opinions that people hold very strongly. For example, the belief that cheating is wrong is a value that many people share. If you believe in this value, you will probably get into a conflict with a friend who wants you to pass him the answers for a test. Values conflicts can be hard to resolve. It's important to stick by your values, especially in situations that involve things that are illegal, dangerous, or just plain wrong. Often the best way out of a values conflict is for both sides to agree to disagree. They can talk with each other to learn each other's views; then they can simply accept the fact that they see things differently.

Possessions—An example of this kind of conflict would be two students fighting over a certain object, like a shared school laptop, or two kids bickering over the last slice of pizza. Both people involved in the conflict want the same thing, but there's not enough for both.

Psychological Needs—Respect, acceptance, control, independence, belonging, friendship—these are all psychological needs. When people feel that these needs aren't being met or are being ignored, a conflict may develop. In a school environment, many conflicts are started because students who gossip spread false or exaggerated rumors about other students, or students are excluded from popular groups. Other conflicts can occur when students begin dating and socializing outside of the school setting.

Most conflicts do not fit into one category. It can take a bit of digging to determine the origin of a conflict, especially if it has many underlining causes. If people don't deal with the underlying cause they won't solve their problems.

Conflict Resolution Skills

Conflict resolution programs help you think about what you usually do when you're involved in a conflict. They can help you understand what changes you might want to make so that conflict solving can become easier. Below are some common ways that people react to conflict:

- Blast it. Some people see conflict as a win-lose situation. They feel that only they are right; the other side is wrong. They try to blast their way through a conflict so that they win and the other side loses. Some do that by fighting. Some overpower the other side with insults, putdowns, bribes, or threats.

- Avoid it. Some people believe that conflict is bad and try to avoid it as much as possible. When a conflict comes up, they may pretend it didn't really happen, or they may always give in and smooth things over. That may make things better for a while, but in the long run, it may actually make them worse.

- Solve it. Instead of ducking conflicts or blasting their way out of them, some people try to face conflicts fairly. They don't try to "win." Instead, they look for the cause of the conflict. Then they try to find a solution that will work well for both parties. Conflict resolution programs encourage people to react in this problem-solving way.

Conflicts can worsen if the people involved yell and scream, or start throwing punches. But they can also get out of control if other people intrude and start taking sides. A crowd of onlookers can make it hard to think calmly. The people having the conflict are supposed to find enough peace to communicate. If they bring in anyone to help, it should be a trained mediator.

Keeping Offensive Language in Check

Saying things such as "You are so rude!" or "You say the dumbest things!" will not be very useful when trying to resolve a conflict. Conflict resolution programs teach people skills to help them keep discussions from turning into putdown sessions.

To communicate more effectively, you need to determine exactly how you feel and why. Then you should explain how you feel using "I" as the first word in your statement. This gives you a chance to state your feelings clearly and calmly, and explain why there is a conflict. You might say, "I feel frustrated because…" or "I am angry because…", and then follow with a specific reason for your frustration or anger. Direct statements such as these keep the discussion focused on the problem. You may be able to compromise to solve the conflict.

The third part of the "I" message, the explanation, helps keep the discussion on target. You're not just making a wild charge. You're backing it up with a clear explanation of how the other person's actions affect you. To do that, you have to think about the situation. Focusing on the problem at hand and not reacting too emotionally can help calm you down and give you time to gain perspective. It can also keep you from blowing things out of proportion. Finally, offer a solution to the conflict and give the other person involved time to respond. Listen to his or her comments and suggestions for resolving the conflict.

Effective Listening

Carefully listening to the other person in a conflict is just as important as stating your own views. Conflict resolution programs try to turn people into active listeners. You also

Listening skills are vital in resolving a conflict. Practice listening skills in the classroom by paying close attention to someone's explanation of an assignment or project.

show the other person you're paying close attention. You let the person know you hear and understand what's being said.

To practice active listening skills, face the person and make eye contact. Don't interrupt when he or she is speaking. While listening, you're supposed to focus on what the other person is saying. Encourage the person to continue talking. You can do this by nodding your head, or saying something like, "Uh-huh." You might ask questions to indicate your interest, or request more information about the situation, such as "How did you feel about that?"

When the person pauses, you should sum up in your own words what was just said. You could begin by responding, "You think what went wrong was…" This process of talking and listening helps prevent further misunderstandings.

Even though you may not agree with the person's views, now is not the time for your opinions. In an effective discussion, both sides take turns speaking. You'll get time to present your views.

Restating what the other person has said lets the person know you listened. It shows you really want to understand, which might calm an angry person. You can also show that you care about how the person feels.

After the person has finished presenting his or her case, you should sum it up by phrasing the problem in your own words. Afterward, you'll get a chance to talk while the other person does the listening.

Another Point of View

If you lose your temper and get into a shouting match with someone, stop the argument before it gets you or the other person to the boiling point. Walk away and take some time to gather your thoughts. This will give you a chance to consider the other person's point of view.

Two people can see the exact same thing and have totally different ideas about it. One example is a basketball game where fans of the winning team are pleased, while fans of the losing team are saddened by the loss. Differences in viewpoint can come from different life experiences.

Learning Some Additional Skills

Some programs teach people how to handle anger in a positive way. One method of learning to manage your anger is to explore what kinds of events trigger it and how to express your feelings without allowing them to get out of hand. One of the main suggestions is to keep your explanation clear and to the point. Don't exaggerate.

Another important skill is being able to comment on someone's idea without criticizing the person. You want to keep focused on the conflict or idea, not the person. You may not agree with what the other person suggests, but the trick is to learn how to disagree diplomatically. Talking about your concerns will help you find a solution or think of a compromise.

chapter five

Peer Mediation

A study published in 2010 by the CDC found that nationwide, 17.5 percent of high school students carried a weapon to school on at least one day during the month before the survey. School officials realized that they had to help students learn better ways to handle problems. More and more schools began to teach nonviolent methods of solving conflicts.

Today, there are thousands of schools across the United States that offer programs in conflict resolution.

In some schools, every student learns the skills of conflict resolution. They do this either in a special class or as part of a regular subject, such as health, English, social studies, or even art.

Other schools involve students in conflict resolution through a peer mediation project. Students act as mediators when their peers (other students) have conflicts they can't solve on their own.

Some schools offer both kinds of programs—conflict resolution classes for everyone, as well as special training for peer mediators. Students in some schools have formed drama groups that spread the word by doing nonviolent problem-solving skits for other students.

Learning is lively in conflict resolution classes. Students don't just sit and listen to lectures. They have to participate. They practice the new skills they're learning by doing skits or by role-playing. Instructors may set up pretend conflict situations and have students act them out, trying different ways to solve the conflict. Or students may work in small discussion groups to test their new skills. Students also get to explore their feelings about conflicts and discuss freely their ideas on many important issues.

Finding Solutions Through Peer Mediation

Some conflicts are too difficult for the people involved to solve on their own. In many schools, conflicts such as these are solved through peer mediation. Specially trained stu-

In this Illinois high school, the peer mediation team members are selected from the student body. The program involves two mediators, a teacher or counselor, and a silent observer who sit down with the two sides to resolve the conflict.

dents called mediators help other students solve problems. In some schools, mediators are known as conflict managers.

Mediators bring together the people who are in conflict for a face-to-face meeting, often called a mediation session. Mediators don't take sides. Instead, they encourage the people involved to discuss things in order to find a solution that is useful for both sides. Mediation sessions are confidential, so everything said is kept private. The people involved feel free to talk knowing that their comments won't be repeated. However, there can be a few exceptions to this rule. For example, if someone threatens suicide, the mediators must notify school officials.

Mediation sessions usually take place in a quiet, private room in school at lunchtime or during free periods. Usually, two student mediators or conflict managers meet with the students who have the conflict, often with a faculty adviser present to observe.

Conflicts can come to mediation in several ways. Bickering students may ask to have their conflict mediated. A teacher may break up a fight in a hallway and refer the battlers to mediation. Or a student conflict manager may stop a fight before it gets out of hand and march the kids down to the mediation room. In some schools, students who get into fights are given a choice: try mediation or face suspension. Some conflicts that student mediators don't handle include those that involve weapons, drugs, or other illegal activities. These situations are referred to adults.

The Peer Mediation Process

At the start of a session, the mediators explain the rules. These usually include: take turns talking, no interrupting, stay seated, and no name-calling. Then each person gets a chance to tell his or her side of the story. To keep the discussion going, mediators listen closely and restate now and then what each person has said. They may also ask questions such as, "How did that make you feel?" or "What else happened?" The mediators don't give suggestions or opinions. Their job is to help the students work together to solve the conflict.

When both sides have had their say, the mediators sum up each side's opinion. They try to get each person to understand the other's point of view. Then both sides conduct a brainstorming session. What are the proposed solutions or compromises? The mediators examine each suggestion. They encourage the people to choose a solution that meets everyone's needs and makes them feel satisfied.

Sometimes the agreement is written down and both people sign it. Other times they just shake on it. Often the mediators set a time to check with both parties later to see if the agreement is still working. If it isn't, the mediators may set up a new session so that all involved can work out a new solution.

School officials report that peer mediation works well. The fact that the sessions are run by students plays a big role. Young people often feel more comfortable sharing their feelings with their peers than with adults. Also important is that someone is really paying attention to what the young people have to say. That alone can reduce anger.

Mediators

Some schools ask students to recommend members of the student body who they would trust to be mediators. Students apply for the position and are interviewed by the faculty advisor or by students already serving as mediators. School officials may appoint students to be mediators.

Mediators should be good listeners. They should also be good talkers, since they have to sum up and restate what both sides say. They have to promise to keep private what's said at a mediation session. Mediators also need to be able to encourage others to open up and say what's on their minds.

Popular and successful students often make good mediators, as do students who have experienced trouble themselves. Sometimes students who have had a conflict mediated appreciate the experience so much that they sign up to be mediators themselves.

Student mediators or conflict managers get special training. They usually attend a series of workshops or classes in which they learn about the causes of conflict, basic conflict resolution skills, and the rules and steps to follow in mediation.

The best part of conflict resolution is resolution. When you use conflict resolution correctly, all of the people involved come out ahead because the solution to the problem meets everyone's needs.

active listening A method of listening in which the listeners show they are paying close attention by making eye contact and restating what other people said.

aggravated assault The crime of physically attacking someone, which results in serious bodily harm and is committed with a weapon.

aggressor A person who attacks or threatens another person.

anonymously Secretly.

brainstorm To come up with many different ideas about a topic.

confidential Private or secret.

confiscate To take away property.

conflict A struggle, quarrel, disagreement, or battle.

conflict manager A person who acts as a mediator to help two sides resolve a conflict.

conflict resolution A method of handling conflicts that encourages people to talk problems out.

diplomatically Relating to dealing with people in a sensitive and effective way.

domestic abuse The use of violence or hurtful words by one family member against another.

"I" message A method of explaining how you feel about something by making a statement that starts with the word "I."

mediation The act of coming between two parties to try to help them resolve a conflict.

mediator A specially trained person who comes between two sides to help them resolve a conflict; a conflict manager.

negotiate To try to settle a conflict by talking, discussing, or compromising.

peer mediation An effort by young people to help other young people resolve a dispute.

psychological Having to do with one's feelings and thoughts.

resolution Dealing with a dispute successfully.

values Ideas a person believes in strongly, such as stealing is wrong.

violence The use of physical force to cause harm.

weapons Guns, knives, pipes, or other items used to cause injury or damage.

zero tolerance A policy used by schools to discipline and punish students for violent offenses.

Brady Center to Prevent Gun Violence
1225 Eye Street NW, Suite 1100
Washington, DC 20005
(202) 898-0792
Web site: http://www.bradycenter.org
The Brady Center is the largest nonpartisan, grassroots
    organization to prevent gun violence. It works to
    educate the public about gun violence and enforce
    regulations to reduce gun violence by attempting to
    regulate the gun industry.

Center for the Prevention of School Violence
1805 Mail Service Center
Raleigh, NC 27699-1805
(800) 299-6054
Web site: http://www.ncdjjdp.org/cpsv
The Center for the Prevention of School Violence serves
    as a resource center that promotes safer schools and
    positive youth development.

Center to Prevent Youth Violence (CPYV)
100 Wall Street, 2nd Floor
New York, NY 10005
(212) 269-5100
Web site: http://www.cpyv.org
The CPYV, formerly known as PAX, is an organization
    whose goal is to end the crisis of youth violence in
    the United States.

National Association of Students Against Violence
    Everywhere (SAVE)

322 Chapanoke Road, Suite 110
Raleigh, NC 27603
(866) 343-SAVE (343-7283)
Web site: http://www.nationalsave.org
SAVE is a student-driven organization that teaches
    crime prevention and conflict management skills,
    and the virtues of good citizenship, civility, and
    nonviolence.

National School Safety Center
141 Duesenberg Drive, Suite 7B
Westlake Village, CA 91362
(805) 373-9977
Web site: http://www.schoolsafety.us
This center helps educate people on violence in U.S.
    schools and makes literature and videos available on
    topics such as school safety, bullies in the classroom,
    and school crime.

National Youth Violence Prevention Campaign
303 Crossways Park Drive
Woddbury, NY 11797
(800) 99-YOUTH (999-6884)
Web site: http://www.nyvpw.org
The goal of this campaign is to raise awareness and educate
    students, teachers, school administrators, counselors,
    school resource officers, school staff, parents, and the
    public on effective ways to prevent or reduce youth
    violence.

National Youth Violence Prevention Resource Center
     (NYVPRC)
P.O. Box 10809
Rockville, MD 20849-0809
(866) SAFE-YOUTH (723-3968)
Web site: http://www.safeyouth.org
The NYVPRC was formed as a single point of access to
     federal information on youth violence.

Public Safety Canada
Minister of Public Safety
House of Commons
Ottawa, ON K1A 0A6
Canada
(800) 830-3118
Web site: http://www.publicsafety.gc.ca
Public Safety Canada is a government-run Web site that
     informs the public about various topics relating to
     safety, including school violence.

Web Sites

Due to the changing nature of Internet links, Rosen
Publishing has developed an online list of Web sites
related to the subject of this book. This site is updated
regularly. Please use this link to access the list:

http://www.rosenlinks.com/tmh/svcr

for further reading

Almond, Lucinda. *School Violence* (Current Controversies). Farmington Hills, MI: Greenhaven Press, 2007.

Atkins, Beth S. *Gunstories: Life-Changing Experiences with Guns*. New York. NY: Katherine Tegen Books, 2006.

Brezina, Corona. *Deadly School and Campus Violence* (Violence and Society). New York, NY: Rosen Publishing Group, 2009.

Brown, Jennifer. *Hate List*. New York, NY: Little, Brown Books for Young Readers, 2010.

Canfield, Jack, and Mark Victor Hansen. *Chicken Soup for the Soul: Teens Talk Tough Times; Stories About the Hardest Part of Being a Teenager*. Cos Cob, CT: Chicken Soup for the Soul Publishing, 2009.

Daniels, Peggy. *School Violence* (Issues That Concern You). Farmington Hills, MI: Greenhaven Press, 2008.

Gimpel, Diane Marczely. *The Columbine Shootings* (Essential Events). San Francisco, CA: Essential Library, 2012.

Hunnicutt, Susan C. *School Shootings* (At Issue). Farmington Hills, MI: Greenhaven Press, 2006.

Lansford, Tom. *Conflict Resolution* (Opposing Viewpoints). Farmington Hills, MI: Greenhaven Press, 2008.

Parks, Peggy J. *School Violence: Current Issues* (Compact Research), San Diego, CA: Referencepoint Press, 2008.

Picoult, Jodi. *Nineteen Minutes: A Novel*. New York, NY: Atria Books, 2007.

Sande, Ken, and Kevin Johnson. *The Peacemaker: Handling Conflict Without Fighting Back or Running Away*. Student Ed. Grand Rapids, MI: Baker Books, 2008.

Schier, Helga. *The Causes of School Violence* (Essential Viewpoints). Minneapolis, MN: ABDO Publishing, 2008.

index

About the Authors

Marilyn E. Smith is a former teacher's assistant. She lives in Michigan.

Matthew Monteverde has a degree in sociology from Rutgers University and writes books for teens. He resides in New Jersey.

Henrietta M. Lily has written several books for young adults, including *Dating Violence* in the Teen Mental Health series. She lives in New York.

Photo Credits

Cover, p. 1 (girls) © istockphoto.com/zorani; cover insets, p. 1 (top) © istockphoto.com/monkeybusinessimages; (middle) © istockphoto .com/Arthur Kwiatkowski; (bottom) © istockphoto.com/jabejon; pp. 1, 3, back cover (head and brain) © istockphoto.com/ Vasily Yakobchuk: p. 3 (laptop) istockphoto.com/Doug De Suza; p. 4 (girl) © istockphoto.com/Steve Debenport; pp. 4, 10, 20, 26, 35 © istockphoto .com/Max Delson Martins Santos; pp. 5, 23, 37 © AP Images; p. 7 © Dick Blume/Syracuse Newspapers/The Image Works; p. 10 © istockphoto.com/drbimages; p. 11 Shelly Katz/Time & Life Images/ Time & Life Pictures/Getty Images; p. 13 © Melanie Stetson Freeman/Christian Science Monitor/The Image Works; p. 16 Image Source/Getty Images; p. 18 © photothek/ullstein bild/The Image Works; p. 20 © istockphoto.com/Juan Estey; p. 22 Robert Nickelsberg/ Getty Images; p. 26 © istockphoto.com/Linda Kloosterhof; p. 27 Weston Colton/Getty Images; p. 32 Creatas Images/Creatas/ Thinkstock; p. 35 © istockphoto.com/Photomorphic Pte Ltd; interior graphics (books) © istockphoto.com/Michal Koziarski.

Designer: Nicole Russo; Photo Researcher: Marty Levick